The M

Written by
Jill Atkins

Illustrated by
Tracy Cottingham

Ransom

Viv has a big pot.

The big pot has no lid.

Will Viv tip red jam in the pot?

Viv tips a tub of red jam in the pot.

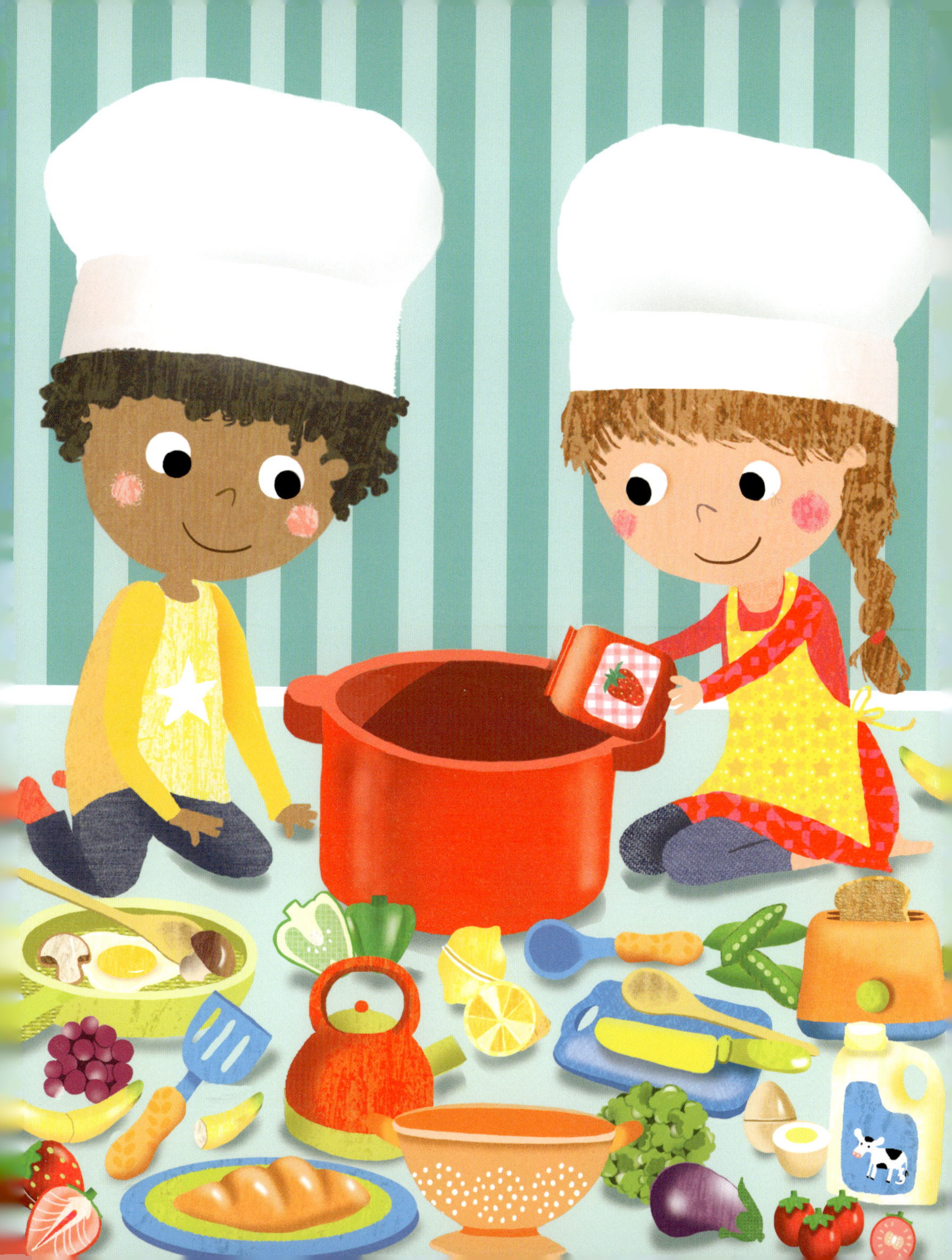

Will Jax tip a bag of nuts in the pot?

Jax tips a bag of nuts in the pot.

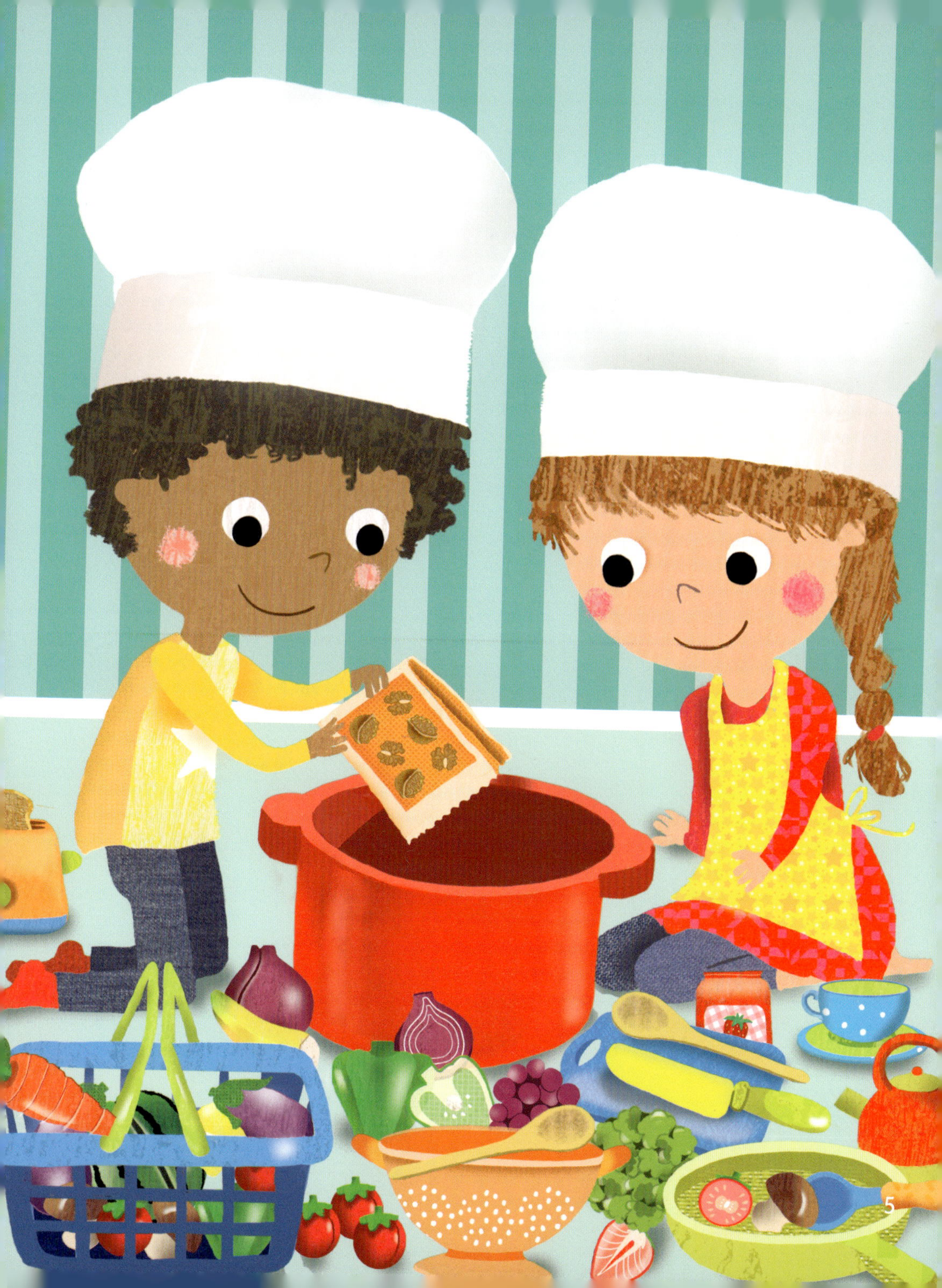

Viv cuts a carrot into six bits.

The carrot will go in the pot.

Jax cuts a melon into ten bits.

The melon will go in the pot.

Viv can mix it up.
Mix, mix, mix!

Jax can mix it up.
Mix, mix, mix!

Let the pot get hot.

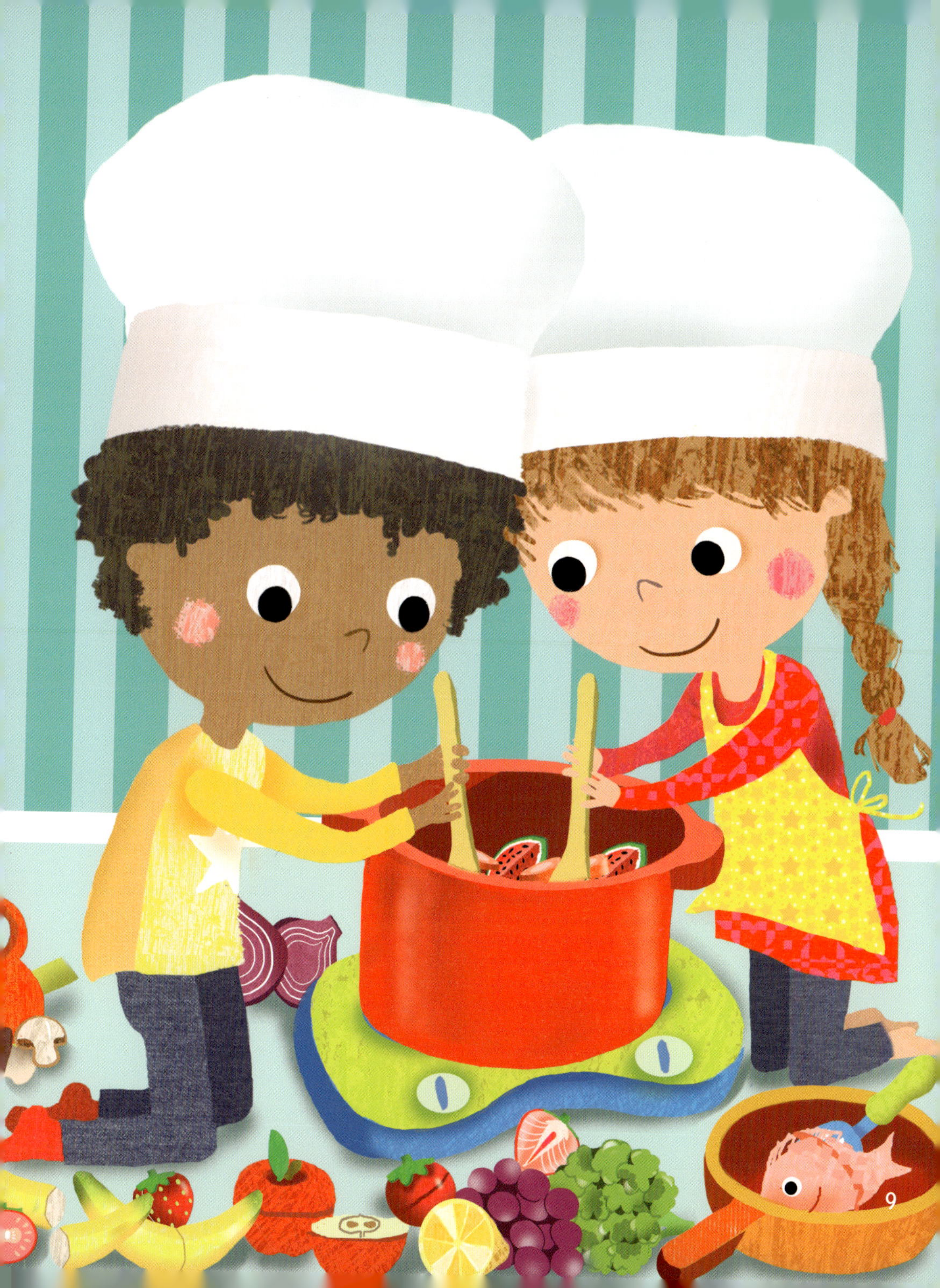

Jax licks his lips.

Jax and Viv sit back and sip the mix.

Is it a top mix?

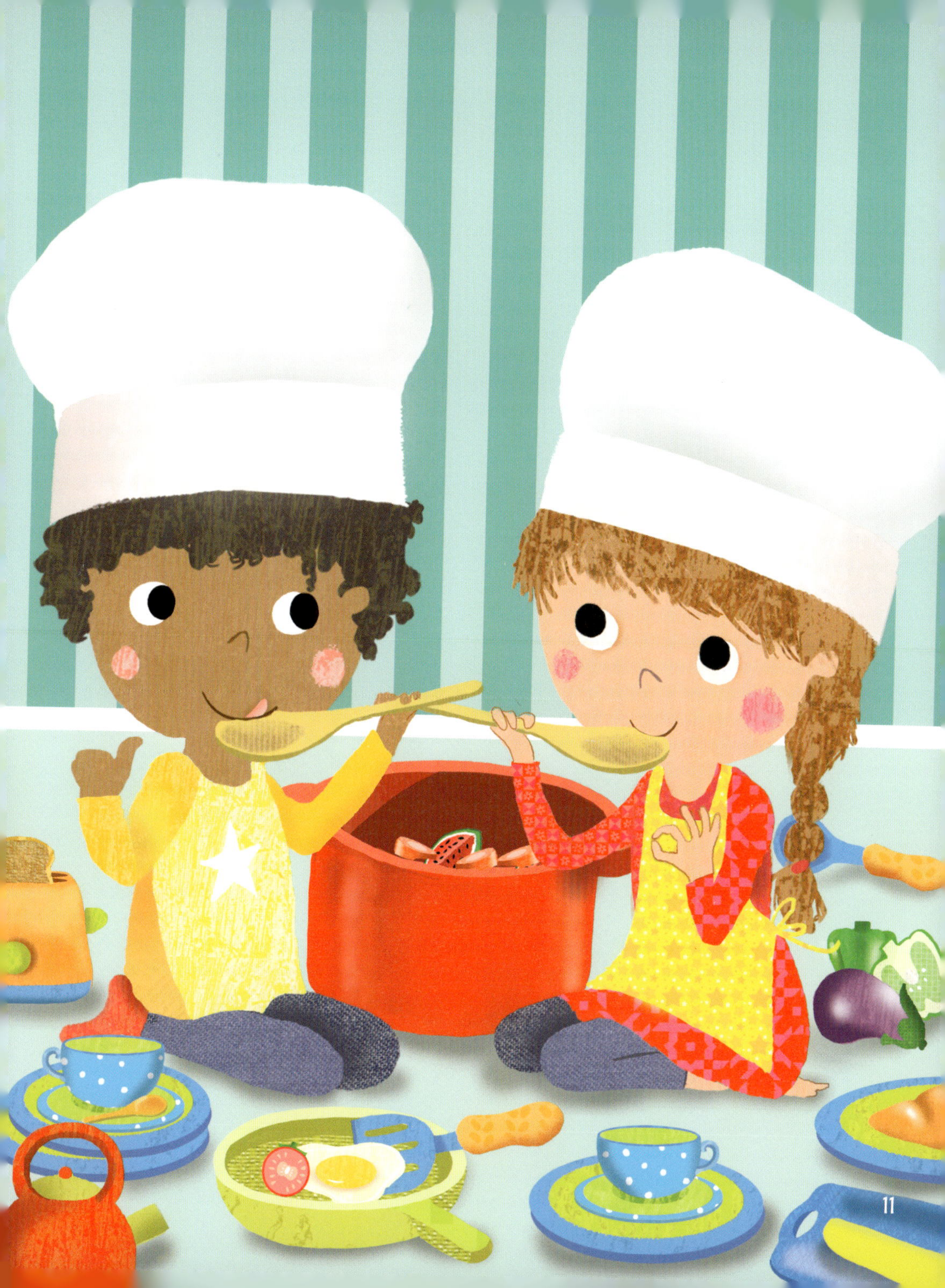

Mum sips a cup of the mix.

It **is** a top mix!